This book belongs to

_____

This book is dedicated to my children - Mikey, Kobe, and Jojo.
Remember to start each day with a positive thought and a grateful heart.

Ninja Life Hacks™

Positive Ninja

Do you think this glass is half full or half empty?

By Mary Nhin

Pictures by
Jelena Stupar

Positivity is a really great thing! It helps to keep me happy. And I like to look on the bright side of things.

For example...

When I accidentally stepped in rain puddles,
I would simply say...

If my pencil broke while I was
drawing, I would think...

I love being positive, but I haven't always known how to be optimistic.

Once upon a time, I really could be quite negative.

At a soccer game, I would scream...

During piano practice, I would shout...

While doing homework, I would say...

Until one day, my friend, Kind Ninja, suggested that I try a fun way to change my thinking. "Do you want me to show you?"

Now, you have room for positive thoughts like...

So I tried it.

I caught my negative thoughts and blew them into a balloon.

It worked! From that day on, I felt a lot less negative and a whole lot happier.

Using this balloon strategy could be your secret weapon against negative thoughts.

Download your Positive Ninja Lesson Plan at NinjaLifeHacks.tv

CPSIA information can be obtained
at www.ICGtesting.com
Printed in the USA
LVHW072015150621
690290LV00007B/353